Tales of Beauty

Retold Timeless Classics

Perfection Learning®

Retold by L. L. Owens

Editor: Susan Sexton
Illustrator: Sue Cornelison

For information, contact:
Perfection Learning® Corporation
Phone: 1-800-831-4190 • Fax: 1-712-644-2392
1000 North Second Avenue, P.O. Box 500
Logan, Iowa 51546-1099

PB ISBN-10: 0-7891-2326-6 ISBN-13: 978-0-7891-2326-8
RLB ISBN-10: 0-7807-7747-6 ISBN-13: 978-0-7807-7747-7
Printed in the U.S.A.

6 7 8 9 10 11 12 13 14 PP 15 14 13 12 11 10 09

Table of Contents

This classic French fable examines the nature of true love.

Beauty and the Beast

A tale from Madame de Villeneuve

Long, long ago, a rich merchant lived in a great mansion. He had three sons and three daughters. The family had everything. Everything, that is, until one unlucky day.

Tragedy Strikes

Out of the blue, the merchant lost his entire fortune.

The merchant was heartbroken. He had worked very hard all of his life. And now the only thing he had left was a tiny cottage in the country. So he and his children went to live there.

On moving day, the family trudged through the dark forest. They walked and walked for what seemed like hours. They finally arrived at its broken-down little door. None of the children had ever seen the cottage. So they were shocked at what they found.

"Oh, Father!" exclaimed the eldest daughter. "This is not at all what we are used to!"

"I know, my child," replied the merchant. "But it is all we have. And we must make the best of it."

"How will we eat?" asked the eldest son.

"You boys will help me farm the land," said the merchant. "You'll have to learn to hunt too. I used to hunt when I was a boy. So I can show you how.

"And you girls," said the merchant, "will have to help too."

"Ugh!" cried all but one of the children.

The youngest child was a girl. She simply said, "We'll do whatever we can, Father."

This young girl's name was Beauty. She was the kindest, sweetest girl you'd ever want to meet. And she was by far the most beautiful girl in the land. She was just like her mother, who'd passed away at Beauty's birth.

Beauty's comment drew angry looks from her brothers and sisters. They were sick and tired of Beauty's goodness. She always did the right thing. Because of this, they always looked selfish.

The merchant was very proud of his youngest child.

"You are just like your mother, my Beauty!" exclaimed the merchant. "I could always count on her. And I can always count on you.

"As for the rest of you," he continued, shaking his head. "You will get used to hard work. You'll have to. Who knows—you may even come to like it!"

Many months came and went. Then the merchant received some good news. His richest ship—once declared lost at sea—had come to port. And he decided to claim it.

"Well, children, I'm off!" exclaimed the merchant. "I'll return in a few days with my fortune. Soon we will be able to return to town and the life we once knew."

"Hooray!" cheered the children. Then they danced about the room.

"To show my appreciation," interrupted the merchant, "I'd like to bring back a gift for each of you. You've all worked so hard this year."

Each child knew exactly what to ask for. All at once, the children shouted—

"I need a velvet coat with topaz buttons!"

"I'll take a bowl filled with gold!"

"Bring me a silver sword!"

"I must have a fur-trimmed gown!"

"Get me a priceless painting!"

The merchant smiled and said, "Done." Then he turned to Beauty, who hadn't chimed in with the others.

"Beauty, my darling, tell me," said the merchant. "What is the one thing you wish for?"

In a soft voice, Beauty said, "All I wish for, dear Father, is your safe return."

Beauty's brothers and sisters all rolled their eyes. One sister guffawed. Another even stuck out her tongue.

"Come on, Beauty," said the eldest sister. "Father wants to share his good fortune with all of us. So choose something. Now."

"She's right, dear," began the merchant. He was quite aware of his other children's selfishness. But he really did want to reward everyone. "Surely you can think of something."

Beauty thought for a long moment. Finally, she said, "I would like a single red rose. You know how much I love roses. And I can't seem to grow them out here in the forest."

"As you wish, Beauty," said the merchant. "I'll bring you the most magnificent red rose in the world."

As he left the cottage, the merchant said, "Farewell to all!"

 ## The Merchant Takes a Trip

The merchant and his horse trotted through the forest and into town. When he arrived at the docks, the merchant found his ship. But thieves had taken everything!

So with a heavy heart, the merchant turned around to go home. "How will I ever tell the children?" he sighed.

Halfway home, a great storm blew in. Blinding snow and cutting winds made it impossible for the merchant to go on. He tied up his horse and crawled into a hollow tree trunk. He covered his head with a blanket. He shook and shivered in the cold. And he wished for the storm to pass.

Soon the merchant fell into a deep sleep. He dreamed of a warm bed and a hearty meal.

When he awoke, the merchant rubbed his eyes. He felt wonderful—all warm and snug. Upon looking around, he gasped, "Where am I?"

For he was in a warm bed. And a piping hot meal was on a tray in front of him. Quickly, he got out of bed and looked out the window. He could see that he was in a great palace on a sunny hill. There were no snowstorms here.

"I do not know how I got here," said the merchant. "But I must find my host and thank him."

As soon as he finished eating, the merchant set out to find the owner of the palace. He searched and searched. But he found no one.

"I'll just have to leave a note," said the merchant at last. "I simply must get back to my children."

The merchant wrote a heartfelt thank-you to his host.

> Dearest Host,
>
> I thank you from the bottom of my heart. Your hospitality knows no bounds. I surely would have frozen to death in that tree trunk. You saved my life. And I am in your debt forever.
>
> Humbly yours,
> The merchant you rescued from the storm

That done, the merchant found his horse and rode toward the palace gates. He passed the most glorious rose garden he had ever seen. And he remembered his promise to Beauty.

"I fear that I cannot honor my promises to the other children," he said sadly. "But I can take a single rose to my youngest daughter."

He picked out a lovely red rose. The moment he plucked it, a big voice boomed, "Thief!"

The man whirled around in alarm. He found himself face-to-face with a most unpleasant creature. It seemed to be a man and a lion and a goat—all rolled into one!

"How dare you take what I do not offer!" roared the beast.

"I-I-I-I'm so s-s-s-sorry," stammered the merchant. "I didn't think you would miss a single rose."

An ugly silence met the scared man's excuse.

Nervously, the merchant began to talk. He told all about losing his fortune. And about learning that his ship had come in. And then finding that it had been robbed. Finally, after thanking the creature for rescuing him, the merchant explained one more thing. He told the great creature why he'd taken the rose. He spoke of his good daughter, Beauty. And of his wish to make her happy.

The creature was a stern one, to be sure. But the tale of young Beauty captured his attention. He paced for a few moments while he thought. Then he spoke.

"You must convince Beauty to visit me. Then your crime will go unpunished. And your fortune will be restored," said the creature.

"What if she won't visit you?" asked the merchant.

"Then you will come back here and be my prisoner forever," replied the creature.

"I'll tell my daughter of your request," said the merchant. "But I won't encourage her to honor it. No father would ask that of his child."

"Be sure to tell her that I am very eager to meet her," urged the creature.

"May I give her your name?" asked the merchant.

The creature paused. Then he declared with a sneer, "Tell your Beauty that my name is Beast."

With great dread, the merchant returned home. Right away, his children knew something was wrong. And they were concerned. Then they heard of Beast's request, and they had much to say.

"Beauty must go there," proclaimed the middle daughter.

"It's for the good of the family," the eldest son added.

"We can move back to town!" cried the eldest daughter, a bit too cheerfully.

This last remark caused everyone to stop and look at Beauty.

"I'm sorry, Beauty," said the youngest son meekly. "It's either you or our poor father."

"I will go," declared Beauty. She'd made up her mind even before her brothers and sisters had spoken. "I am not afraid of this creature called Beast."

Beauty's father tried to talk her out of going. For he did not want any harm to come to her. But it was no use. Beauty was going to visit Beast. And that was that.

Beauty Meets Beast

No sooner did Beauty begin her journey than she was swept inside Beast's palace. In the Beast's palace, Beauty's chamber was filled with red roses. All around her were gifts. New dresses. Fine food. Precious gems.

Meanwhile, back home, Beauty's family had been whisked to their old mansion. Their house was brimming with riches and feasts fit for royalty!

Beauty took a moment to catch her breath. Bravely, she looked around and said, "My name is Beauty. I have come to meet Beast. Please show yourself to me."

Beast appeared in a puff of smoke. Beauty was afraid of his ugliness. But she tried not to show it.

"Do you like what you see, young lady?" asked Beast.

Beauty could not lie. So she said, "This room is delightful. And the dresses are divine."

"Ha!" shrieked Beast. "A clever girl you are! I shall enjoy talking with you. And soon, you shall agree to be my wife."

Beauty was sure that she could never agree to such a thing. But she kept quiet for now. She did not wish to anger Beast.

Weeks and months passed. And Beauty was able to amuse herself with the palace's many luxuries. Beast had endless gardens for Beauty to walk through. His library was filled with every book ever written. And he had a room filled with all the musical instruments ever invented.

If Beauty got bored, she could always go to the game room. Or the weaving room. A particular favorite of hers was the theater. Actors and mimes acted out sweet plays—just for her.

Each evening after supper, Beast called Beauty to his parlor. There he spun magical tales of a handsome young prince. He would speak for hours about this prince's glorious life. Beauty loved to listen.

Beauty became very fond of Beast. He liked to act tough. But through his stories, Beauty saw that he was not evil at heart. He was just sad and lonely. And he truly longed for a different life. Like the one of the prince in his stories.

Before saying good night one evening, Beast became very serious.

"Beauty," he began. "I feel the time has come for me to ask you something. Something very important."

"What is it, Beast?" asked Beauty. "You can ask me anything."

"We shall see," said Beast, hesitating. "Now promise not to fear giving me your honest answer."

"I could never fear you, dear friend," laughed Beauty. "Maybe I did once . . . but I don't anymore."

"Very well," nodded Beast. Then he bowed to Beauty and asked, "Will you marry me?"

"Oh, Beast, I'm afraid I cannot," Beauty said, shaking her head. "You see, I am waiting for my true love to find me."

"I do not understand," Beast sighed. Clearly, his feelings were hurt. "Do you not smile when I greet you every day? Do you not enjoy spending time with me? Do you not laugh at my jokes? And do you not comfort me when I am glum?"

Beauty was confused. Beast was right about all those things. Even so, Beauty felt in her heart that her true love would appear one day. So she had no choice but to refuse Beast's proposal.

"I'm sorry, Beast," Beauty said. "We must remain friends—and friends only."

Beast was crushed. But he was able to go on. Because, deep down, he really believed that Beauty loved him.

Somehow, I will make her see it, Beast thought to himself.

Beauty's life at the palace continued. She spent her days reading and playing and singing. And she spent her evenings talking with Beast. She quite enjoyed herself. The only thing she missed was her family.

Beauty often found herself begging Beast to share more stories about the prince. She secretly hoped to meet him. For she thought that he might be her true love.

As Beauty dreamed one starry night, the young prince spoke to her. He whispered, "Do not be blind to what you cannot see. Let your heart be your guide."

When Beauty awoke, she remembered the prince's words. She thought about them all day. But she did not understand.

I'll figure it out soon enough, Beauty thought. Perhaps my prince will explain it to me himself.

Perhaps he would, indeed!

The next afternoon was sunny and clear. Beast appeared in the garden where Beauty was walking. Beauty was surprised. Because Beast usually only showed himself in the evening. He felt that candlelight and moonglow softened his looks.

"Why, hello there!" said a startled Beauty. "It's lovely to see you this afternoon. Is everything all right?"

Beast assured her that all was well. Then he asked her to sit down on a marble bench.

"I know how you long to see your family, Beauty," began Beast.

"You are right," she agreed. "It is my heart's desire to see them again."

"I want you to be happy," said Beast. "So I am sending you to your father's house for a visit."

"How wonderful! Thank you!" cried Beauty. "When will I go?"

"You will leave now," answered Beast. "But before you go, I must ask. Will you marry me?"

"Oh, Beast," said Beauty. "I dislike hurting you. You are such a dear, dear friend. And I love you so. But I'm afraid my answer is still no. My true love is out there. He is searching for me. And when he finds me, I must not disappoint him."

"Will you know him when you see him, Beauty?" asked Beast.

"Without a doubt," she answered.

"Very well," said Beast sadly. "You shall leave right now. But you must promise to come back in one week. Otherwise, I shall die of a broken heart."

Beauty vowed to come back.

Beast offered her a heart-shaped locket. Inside was a gleaming diamond.

"Open the locket when you are ready to come back," said Beast. "All you have to do is hold the gem in your hand and wish to see me again."

"I'll see you in one week—I promise," declared Beauty.

With that, Beauty found herself in her family's home. Her father was standing in front of her.

"My precious daughter has returned!"

shouted the merchant. "Oh, happy day!"

The other children gathered around her. Beauty told them all about her time at the palace. In the past, they would have been jealous. But now they were pleased. Beauty's actions had restored their father's wealth. So they welcomed her home and treated her well.

Beauty had a very busy week. She spent long mornings talking with her father. And hectic afternoons meeting her sisters' new friends. In the evenings, she attended charming parties held in her honor. Everyone in town was thrilled to see Beauty back home. And she was happy to be there too.

Beauty Breaks Her Promise

It was finally the seventh night of Beauty's visit. I'll stay just a few more days, she thought. Beast will understand.

On the eighth night, the young prince visited her dreams.

"Where are you, Beauty?" he asked. "I'm waiting for you. But you do not come."

On the tenth night, Beauty again dreamed of the prince. He was lying on Beast's marble bench, moaning and groaning. And he was as pale as a ghost!

"Beauty," he whimpered. "Why did you

19

break your promise? I shall not live to see the next day."

Beauty woke with a start. She could not remember her dream. But something told her that Beast was in danger. Quickly, she pried open her locket. Alas! The diamond had turned to coal!

Beauty rubbed the coal with all her might. And she made a wish.

"Please, please take me to Beast," she begged. "He needs me right away!"

In an instant, Beauty was standing near the marble bench. Beast was lying on his side, clutching his heart.

Through swollen eyes, he saw Beauty. He mumbled, "Ah, my precious Beauty. I must be dreaming."

Beauty knelt near the bench and stroked Beast's matted hair. Softly, she said, "It is not a dream, Beast. I have come back. I will take care of you and make you well."

"So it is you," answered Beast. "You are too late, I fear. You broke your promise. And I am slipping away."

Beauty Sees Her Prince!

Beauty began to weep. Even in his weakened state, Beast tried to comfort her.

Beauty gazed deep into Beast's gentle eyes. To her, Beast looked noble and handsome. More handsome than any prince could, either real or imagined.

This only made Beauty cry harder. For she finally understood what the prince had meant. When he'd said, "Do not be blind to what you cannot see," he was talking about Beast!

"I do not deserve your kindness!" Beauty wailed. "You've been so good to me. So true! All this time, I've been waiting for true love. But it was right in front of me. You were right in front of me!"

Suddenly, millions of shooting stars lit up the sky. Trumpets sounded. And joyful cheers rang through the night air. In a puff of smoke, Beast changed. He became the strong, smiling, handsome prince of Beauty's dreams.

"I have been trapped in an evil spell," he said. "At long last, your love for my inner beauty has set me free."

Beauty did not want to waste another moment. So she asked her prince, "Will you marry me?"

Joyfully, the prince replied, "Yes, I will!"

And the two lived blissfully ever after.

*In this favorite Danish tale, a big,
ugly duckling is teased for being different.
But when he strikes out on his own, he
learns that he is beautiful after all.*

The Ugly Duckling

A tale from Hans Christian Andersen

It was a clear summer day in the country. A lovely old farmhouse stood in a sunny spot. The house was near a deep river. And near the river sat a duck on her nest.

This duck had been waiting and watching for her eggs to hatch. Finally, one shell cracked. Then another. And another.

Three tiny creatures lifted their heads and cried, "Peep-peep-peep!"

"Quack-quack-quack," said the mother. And then they all quacked as well as they could.

The little ones looked about.

"The world is so big," said the ducklings.

The mother told her youngsters all about the land and the river. She shared other knowledge with them too.

After a while, the mother noticed something. Her largest egg had not yet hatched. So she seated herself on the nest at once.

"Oh, my!" she exclaimed. "I hope this duckling hatches soon."

Before long, an old duck stopped by for a visit. She'd heard that the new ducklings had arrived.

"How are you feeling?" asked the old duck.

"I'm just fine, thank you. But look. This egg doesn't seem to want to hatch."

"Oh, yes. I see," said the old duck. "What you have there is a turkey's egg. See how big and gray it is?"

"A turkey's egg?" said the duck. "Don't be ridiculous. This is one of my eggs. Trust me, a mother knows."

"Whatever you say, dear," said the old duck. She wasn't convinced. But she thought it best to drop the subject.

"Have you seen my other ducklings?" asked the mother. "Aren't they the prettiest little things you ever saw?"

"They are darling," agreed the old duck. "Shouldn't you be teaching them to swim now?"

"Not just yet," answered the mother. "I'd like to sit on this egg a bit longer. So that all my precious ducklings can learn to swim together."

"Do what you want," said the old duck. As she waddled away, she muttered, "Too bad turkeys don't like the water."

At last, the big gray egg broke. The duckling cried, "Peep-peep-peep!"

The mother said, "Quack-quack-quaaa—" But she stopped short.

The duckling looked up at her with trusting eyes. "Quack-quack-quack," repeated the duckling.

The mother was stunned. Not by what she heard—but by what she saw. This duckling was very large. And very ugly.

"Well, my goodness!" exclaimed the mother. "What have we here?" She didn't know what else to say. After some thought, she said, "Come and meet the other ducklings."

The next day, the mother took her young ones to the water. She jumped in with a splash.

"Quack-quack-quack!" the mother cried. And all her little ducklings jumped in.

The ducklings bobbed about. Each time their heads disappeared underwater, they popped right back up again. They peeped and quacked with joy at their new adventure. Soon they were all swimming quite gracefully. Especially the ugly duckling.

"Oh, goody!" cheered the mother. And she called the old duck over to take a look.

"See there, old duck," the mother said excitedly. "My youngest duckling cannot be a turkey—he swims so well! And honestly, once you get used to him, he's not so very ugly after all."

"If you say so, dear," replied the old duck.

"Quack-quack-quack!" called the mother to her brood. "Come, children. It is time for you to meet the other animals in the farmyard. I want all of you to be on your best behavior."

And so the group marched across the yard. The ducklings were eager to meet new friends—especially the other ducks.

The other ducks stared as the family approached. "Look," said one duck. "Here comes the new brood. They've certainly got a strange brother."

"What a funny-looking thing," said a mean duck. "We don't want him here!" And he flew out and bit the ugly duckling's leg.

"Ouch!" cried the ugly duckling. "That hurt!"

"Leave him alone," warned the mother. "He did nothing to hurt you."

"But he is so big. And he's the ugliest duckling ever," retorted the mean duck. "We cannot allow him to stay on this farm."

"He is part of my family," said the mother. "And he will stay with me."

After that, the ducklings sang and played and got to know their neighbors. But the ugly duckling had no fun. He was laughed at all day long. The ducks bit him. The chickens pecked at him. And the girl who fed the animals kicked him.

When he could take no more, the ugly duckling decided to run away. "No one will miss me!" he sobbed. He flew and flew as far as he could. He didn't stop until he came to a large moor. Then he huddled up next to a rock and slept through the night.

The next morning, a group of wild ducks found him.

"Are you a duck?" they all said, lining up to see him.

He bowed to them. But he did not answer their question. He didn't know what to do.

"You are terribly ugly," said the wild ducks. "But you may stay here for now. Just don't get in our way."

"Thank you," said the ugly ducking. For two days and nights, he rested on the moor. On the third day, two wild geese happened by.

"Listen, duckling," said one of the geese. "We're flying to another moor today. Would you like to come with us?"

"I'd like that. Thank you," replied the duckling.

So the little party took off. They had flown a just few hundred yards when they heard an awful racket. POP! POP! POP!

Suddenly, the two wild geese fell out of the air and into the stream. The duckling rushed to the water's edge. The water was tinted red with his new friends' blood!

POP! POP! POP! POP! POP! echoed in the distance. And a whole flock of wild geese rose up from the reeds. They shouted to each other, "Run for your lives!"

The ugly duckling heard the sounds of barking hounds. He spotted men in orange jackets scattered about the moor. Some were even stationed in trees. The blue smoke from these hunters' guns floated over the treetops. And the poor duckling was terrified.

At that moment, a mean-looking dog rushed toward the duckling. His big, pink tongue was wagging. And his eyes were narrowed for the hunt. He gave the duckling a quick sniff and a snort. Then he splashed into the water to fetch an injured goose.

"Goodness me," sighed the duckling. He was relieved, though, that the dog had found him too ugly even to bite.

The duckling hid behind a tree for several hours. He didn't dare make a sound. When the shooting and howling died down, he made a decision.

"I must go out into the world again," he declared.

After a day or so, he came upon a pretty blue lake. He plunged in, eager to swim again. The water was so calm and so warm. And soon the duckling was splashing about.

Autumn arrived. And the leaves on the trees turned orange and gold. When the early winds of winter blew the leaves off the trees, the young duckling felt sad.

One crisp evening, he sat shivering in his little home of twigs and leaves. At dusk, a flock of beautiful white birds rose from the bushes. The duckling watched the graceful creatures in wonder. They were swans—with curved necks and silky feathers.

The birds cried out as one and spread their splendid wings. They flew away to warm homes across the sea. As they flew higher and higher, the ugly duckling felt a kinship with them. He paddled into the water, stretched out his neck, and gave a familiar cry. It sounded just like the cry of the swans!

"How I wish I were a swan," said the duckling. He watched and watched until the flock was out of sight.

The days grew shorter and colder. Each day, the duckling's space on the lake became smaller. And before long, it froze hard—with the duckling trapped and helpless. He might have frozen solid himself. But luckily, a kind peasant freed him from his icy prison. And he wrapped him in a warm blanket.

Winter raged on. It was a miserable season for the poor duckling. When it finally passed, the duckling found a nice spot on a moor. The bright sun warmed his feathers. Birds sang happily. And apple trees were in the full bloom of spring.

One day, the young bird felt strong enough to fly. So he flapped his wings and rose high into the sky. He stopped to rest in a large garden. There he saw three white swans swimming in a pond. Cautiously, he dropped into the water and swam to them.

The moment the swans saw him, they rushed to his side.

The poor bird, fearing an attack, hung his head and waited.

But wait! What did he see in the clear water below? Why, it was his own image. And it was that of a magnificent white swan. He'd grown up over the long, hard winter. And he wasn't a duck—or even a turkey—after all!

The other swans greeted the stranger and stroked his neck. "Welcome to our flock!"

Presently, some children skipped into the garden. They threw bits of cake into the water.

A boy cried, "Come see! There is a new one."

The other children were thrilled. And they danced and clapped and sang, "A new swan has arrived!"

"The new swan is the most beautiful of all!" said one of the girls.

The old swans bowed their heads toward the newcomer. He shyly covered his face with his wing. He was confused. All his life, he had been hated for his ugliness. And now others said he was the most beautiful bird of all.

Then a dazzling beam of sunlight washed over him. The swan realized why he had suffered so. And he was grateful. For it made the joy around him seem that much grander.

So he rustled his feathers, curved his slender neck, and cried out to those around him:

"Happiness has found me at last! And I shall cherish it forever!"

*A spoiled young princess hears
a thing or two about the importance of
appearances. Does she get the message?*

The Frog Prince

It was a fair spring evening a long time ago. A young princess played in the woods.

The girl had taken a big red ruby from her mother's dressing table. She tossed it about as if it were an ordinary plaything. Soon, the princess threw the ruby a bit too hard. It sailed past a tree, rolled down a hill, and plopped into the spring.

The princess had lost many things this way. But this was her mother's favorite jewel. She was worried.

"I would give anything to have that ruby back!" she cried.

Just then, an enormous green frog leapt in front of the princess. He croaked, "Hello, beautiful princess. I can fetch your ruby for you. All you have to do is let me live with you in the palace."

What an idiot, thought the princess. I would never let this pitiful creature live with me! But I will play along with him. At least long enough to get my ruby back.

"It is a deal," said the princess. And before she knew it, the frog had retrieved the ruby.

The girl grabbed the gem. Then she ran home as fast as she could. And she slammed the palace doors behind her.

By the next morning, the princess had all but forgotten the frog. She was sitting at the breakfast table when she heard a strange noise. First, there was a thumping sound right outside the window. Then a raspy voice called out to her.

"Young princess! It is me, your friend the frog. The one who did you a favor. You must let me in. You promised I could live with you!"

Now, the king was eating his breakfast too. He asked, "Young lady, is this frog telling the truth? Did you promise to let him live here?"

"I did, Father," answered the princess. "But I never thought he could find his way to the palace from the spring. It's quite a trip for a stubby little frog to make."

"You're right," noted the king. "But a promise is a promise. Haven't I always said so?"

"Yes, Father."

"Then it is settled," declared the king. "The frog stays. Go let him in. Hurry up now!"

Over the next few days, the frog made himself at home. He followed the princess wherever she went, causing her much distress.

"Give me a bite of food from your plate," he'd say. Or, "Let me sleep on your pillow."

The king usually made his daughter honor her guest's requests. Many times, behind the king's back, the frog asked the princess to pick him up and carry him somewhere. But she always refused—and none too politely either!

Finally, the frog went too far. He asked for a kiss, and the girl lost all patience.

"Stop following me around, you wretched, slimy thing!" she screamed. "I've given you food. And I've let you lay your warty head on my pillow. But I will never kiss you! Never!"

The frog just smiled. "Then at least pick me up and take me back to the spring. It is the least you can do to repay your debt to me."

This so angered the princess that she

grabbed the frog and hurled him out the door.

When the frog hit the ground, lightning struck him. And he was no longer a frog. Instead he was a tall, handsome prince.

The princess was astonished! She turned around and rubbed her eyes, then turned around again.

"Where on earth is that awful frog?" she wondered aloud.

The prince answered, "I was that awful frog. Your touch broke the wicked spell that had me trapped. Please accept my thanks."

By this time, the prince's coachman had appeared. "Well, I'm off!" he exclaimed with a wave.

As the prince stepped into his gold carriage, the princess shouted, "Wait!"

"There is something else, milady?" the prince asked.

"Why, yes, sir," the princess said sweetly.

The princess's head was spinning. She had to think of a way to stall the prince—fast. She knew that, as a prince, he would one day be a king. So he would need a queen.

The princess babbled on, "You simply must stay for dinner. My mother and father would love to meet you. We could all get to know each other. Wouldn't that be fun?"

The prince shook his head and replied, "I am sorry, milady. But I cannot accept your invitation."

"I don't understand," pouted the princess.

"Why, only moments ago, you were disgusted with me," explained the prince. "Surely your feelings could not have changed so completely."

"That is not fair," whined the princess. "You did not show your true self to me."

"Ah, but I did—just as you showed your true self to me," the prince answered.

He went on. "You see, I am the same soul who tricked and badgered you. And you are the same nasty girl who flung me out the door."

"But things are different now that I know you're a prince," the princess protested.

"That's right," nodded the prince. "For now, when you look at me, all you see is beauty. And when I look at you, I see none at all."

With that, the prince tapped on the carriage and ordered, "Take me to my homeland!"

The princess watched until the carriage became a dot on the horizon. Then she strolled to the spring. Why? To search for another frog, of course!

This is a German tale
of a prince who uses his special powers
to enchant a beautiful girl and her family.

HÁBOGI

There once was a peasant couple who had three daughters. Inga was the eldest. Marta was next. And Helga was the youngest. As is usually the case, the youngest daughter was the most beautiful. And the sweetest. And when her sisters went out to play, Helga did not. She was always content to stay in and do their chores.

The years passed quickly for the family. One breezy spring evening, Papa suddenly noticed something. It seemed that his girls had turned into spirited young ladies. All three were old enough to marry.

Papa spoke about this to Mama. Mama agreed. She said they should prepare to open their home to suitors.

As the girls flitted about the cottage, Papa teased Inga. "What do you suppose your husband's name is to be?" he asked.

"Oh, Papa," Inga answered, quite seriously. "I simply must marry a man called Sigmund."

"You are in luck then," nodded Papa. "There are a great many Sigmunds nearby to choose from."

Turning to Marta, he said, "What do you say, my dear?"

"Why, Papa, there is no name more beautiful than Sigurd!" she cried.

"Another good choice," said Papa. "For I can think of seven Sigurds in this village alone."

Papa then questioned Helga. "And what about you, my pet? Have you picked out your mate's name?"

Helga smiled. She did have a favorite name. It was Njal. But just as she was going to say it, a strange voice whispered in her ear. It said, "You will marry the one called Hábogi."

How strange, Helga thought as she looked about the room. No one else seems to have heard that. Oh, well. No matter. I have never heard such a name. And I do not like it.

Helga opened her mouth to announce her favorite name. But instead, she said, "My husband will be called Hábogi."

"Hábogi, you say?" asked Papa. "What kind of name is that? I know of no such person. No, there is no one named Hábogi in these parts."

"Indeed, there is not," added Mama. "Surely, Helga, you don't wish to end up an old maid like your Aunt Matilda. So be a good girl and tell us your real answer."

Now Helga was as surprised as anyone at what she'd said. But she was no longer able to control her words. Again, she insisted, "I will marry Hábogi or no one at all."

And that was that.

It wasn't long before the young men in the land had heard of the three girls. Many Sigmunds and Sigurds visited the cottage. Men with different names visited too—even a few Njals. But there were no Hábogis.

Inga chose her Sigmund. And Marta chose her Sigurd. They decided they would have a double wedding. Friends and kinsmen came together for the happy occasion.

As the guests gathered for the ceremony, an ugly, ugly man came out of the crowd. He walked straight over to Papa. "I am Hábogi," he said. "And Helga will marry me."

Helga saw this. She started to tremble. But she did not run away.

Papa was stunned by the man's appearance. The man was terrible—and he seemed so old.

Papa could not bear the thought of giving his lovely young daughter to such an awful-looking creature. Yet the man was so persuasive that Papa couldn't seem to reject him.

So Papa replied, "Off with you, man. I cannot make a decision yet. The wedding is about to begin."

Hábogi stepped back. He said, "Very well. But when the wedding is over, Helga will leave with me."

And so the wedding took place. Afterward, the two sisters had a chance to discuss Helga and Hábogi. You see, they had always been jealous of Helga. So they were quite pleased that Helga might marry the horrible old man.

"Your Sigurd is much handsomer than that awful Hábogi," crowed Inga.

"As is your Sigmund!" cried Marta.

"Poor, dear Helga," began Inga. "How sad that she will end up with that beast."

Inga's words hung in the air for a moment. Then the sisters laughed merrily and skipped back to the party.

After the wedding feast, Hábogi led a fine horse out of a nearby field. The horse had a brilliant saddle of crimson and gold. Helga looked at Hábogi's crooked grin. Then, quite against her wishes, she found herself jumping onto the saddle.

"Where are you taking me?" Helga demanded.

Hábogi noticed Helga's fright. "Don't worry," said he. "You'll see your family again."

"That's no answer," Helga responded.

"I am about to show you your new home," said Hábogi. "I hope you will be pleased."

Hábogi himself mounted the horse. He sat in front of Helga and took the reins. Soon, they had ridden out of sight.

Mama and Papa were alarmed. But they did not go after their sweet daughter.

"I pray she will be safe," said Mama.

"Her future husband will protect her," replied Papa, surprised by his own words.

Meanwhile, Hábogi and Helga's horse galloped across the country. They entered a meadow that had the greenest grass Helga had ever seen.

"Oh, my! Look over there at those fluffy white sheep!" exclaimed Helga.

"The finest sheep in the herd shall be yours, Helga," declared Hábogi. "For this is my meadow—and my herd."

Helga was stunned. She thanked Hábogi for his gift. Soon they were riding through a huge field. It was filled with the most charming gray cows imaginable.

"The milk from those pretty cows must be delicious," said Helga.

"It is," answered Hábogi. "And after we wed, you shall taste the sweetest milk from the finest cow every morning. For this is my field. And these are my cows."

Helga was impressed. But she remained silent. When they reached a valley, Helga nearly sprang out of the saddle. She shrieked with delight when she saw dozens of happy horses at play. There were horses of shiny chestnut, snow white, jet black, and golden yellow.

Helga was breathless with excitement. "Tell me, Hábogi. Do you own these fine horses too?"

"Indeed," said Hábogi. "Which one do you admire most?"

"They are all so lovely," began Helga. "I suppose I would have to choose the jet-black one with the little white star on his forehead. But surely, Hábogi, you don't mean to give me a lamb, a cow, and a horse!"

"Ah, but surely I do, Helga. For you are to be my wife. And what's mine is yours."

Well, Helga didn't know what to think anymore. She was no longer afraid of Hábogi.

However, she couldn't stop thinking about his face. It was so displeasing. Hábogi had caught her staring at him more than once. But he never shrank from her gaze. He just kept guiding the horse farther and farther into the country.

Many miles later, Hábogi stopped the horse. They were in front of a tiny run-down shack.

"Are we lost?" asked Helga. She did not like the looks of this place.

"Not at all," replied Hábogi. "This is my home. Soon it will be your home too."

Hábogi got down first. Then he lifted Helga from the horse. Helga hesitated before taking Hábogi's arm.

This terrible man has tricked me, Helga thought. I believed that he owned all those sheep and cows and horses. But it cannot be true. Just look at this hut. It's practically falling down! What will become of me?

Hábogi led Helga up the steps and through the door. Once she was inside, Helga's jaw dropped. She was blinded by the sparkling beauty of all that surrounded her. There were gold statues and silver baubles. Porcelain figurines and crystal vases. And silk tapestries and cushions. It was too much for Helga to take in.

It will take a long time to study everything, thought Helga.

Hábogi interrupted Helga's thoughts. "It is time for you to go," he said. "I must prepare for our wedding. My servant will take you home. In three days, he will bring you back with your family and your guests."

Helga went with the servant. Her mind raced as they traveled back over the countryside. In no time, she was home.

"My dear, dear girl!" shouted Papa when he saw Helga.

"You've come home to us, my child!" cried Mama.

"Where is your Hábogi?" scoffed Inga.

"Let me guess—he's cast you aside," sneered Marta.

Helga let the questions die down. Then she explained. "I came home to invite you to my wedding. It's in three days."

"But where is Hábogi from?" asked Papa.

"And what does he do?" asked Mama.

"What is he worth?" demanded Inga.

"Do you realize how ugly your children will be?" bellowed Marta.

"You shall learn the answers you seek in three days," said Helga. "I promise."

With that, the subject was closed.

Three days seemed forever to Inga and Marta. The sisters tried everything to get Helga to talk of her time with Hábogi. They asked sweetly. They tried trickery. They even begged. But Helga wouldn't say a word.

Finally, the wedding day arrived. And Helga's party set out. Along the way, Helga pointed out Hábogi's sheep and cows and horses. Inga and Marta were green with envy. But the sight of Hábogi's awful-looking little hut did much to console them.

"Well, well," laughed Inga. "What have we here?"

"What a charming little cottage!" cried Marta. "We're both so happy for you. Aren't we, Inga?"

"Oh, naturally!" Inga could hardly hide her delight.

As the party went inside, though, the sisters were shocked. Never had they seen such finery.

At once, Mama gasped, "The wedding dress!" And everyone's eyes found the glittering gown hanging in the corner. It was beautiful! Yards of flowing white satin were covered with hundreds of tiny, sparkling diamonds and sapphires. It was fit for a princess.

Mama and Papa were delighted. They now felt that Helga would have a good life with Hábogi. Helga was happy too. She couldn't wait to marry Hábogi the next day. The sisters, however, were upset. They hated to think that Helga had found a better match than they had.

So that night, while the rest of the wedding party slept, Marta and Inga came up with a plan.

"Helga does not deserve that dress!" exclaimed Marta.

"How true," declared Inga. "We can't let her look better than we did at our wedding."

"What should we do?" asked Marta.

"We'll destroy her gown," replied Inga. "It's the only way."

By moonlight, the sisters took the dress outside. They found the ash pit.

"This is perfect," they said.

They hurled the gown into the pit and covered it with ashes.

"No one will ever find this," said Inga.

"No one," said Marta.

Now Hábogi had seen the way Marta and Inga treated Helga. He sensed that they were up to no good. So he had kept an eye on them. And at the proper moment, he turned the ashes in the pit to rose petals. (You see, he happened to know some magic.)

When the sisters saw this, they tried to run away. But it was too late. Hábogi had cast a spell over them too. They froze in place and were covered with ashes.

The next morning, the rest of the guests arrived for the wedding. They all passed by the motionless Marta and Inga. Some shouted, "What fools!" Others just pointed and laughed.

Everyone was surprised to see a glorious castle. It was standing where the awful little hut had been. Helga and a handsome prince stood in front of it.

The prince wore a splendid coat of blue velvet and silver trim. On his head was a crown. Helga was radiant in her jeweled gown. And her delicate veil was made of spun gold.

Mama and Papa rushed to Helga's side.
"Who is this man?" they wondered.
"This is my Hábogi," she smiled.

The Play

HÁBOGI

Cast of Characters

Narrator

Papa

Inga

Marta

Mama

Helga

Hábogi

Setting: Springtime in the country

Act I

Narrator: There once was a peasant couple who had three daughters—Inga, Marta, and Helga. Helga, the youngest, was the sweetest and the most beautiful.

One breezy spring evening, Mama and Papa were talking. They suddenly realized that all three of their daughters were old enough to marry. Papa started teasing his girls.

Papa: What do you suppose your husband's name is to be, Inga?

Inga: Oh, Papa. I simply must marry a man called Sigmund.

Papa: You are in luck, then. There are a great many Sigmunds to choose from. What do you say, Marta?

Marta: Why, Papa, there is no name more beautiful than Sigurd!

Mama: Another good choice. Don't you agree, Papa? I can think of as many as seven Sigurds in this village alone!

Papa: And what about you, Helga? Have you picked out your mate's name?

Narrator: Helga smiled. She did have a favorite name. It was Njal. But just as she was going to say it, a strange voice whispered in her ear. It said, "You will marry the one called Hábogi."

Helga thought this was strange. She looked about the room. No one else seemed to have heard that. She began to say that she wished to marry a Njal. But something else came out instead.

Helga: My husband will be named Hábogi.

Papa: *Hábogi,* you say? What kind of name is that? I know of no such person.

Mama: Nor do I. Surely, Helga, you don't wish to end up an old maid like your Aunt Matilda. So be a good girl and tell us your *real* answer.

Narrator: Helga was as surprised as anyone at what she'd said. But she was no longer able to control her words. Again, she insisted—

Helga: All I can say is that I will marry Hábogi. Or no one at all!

Narrator: Soon, many Sigmunds and Sigurds came to visit the girls. Men with different names visited too—even a few Njals. But there were no Hábogis.

Inga chose her Sigmund, and Marta chose her Sigurd. They decided that they would have a double wedding. Friends and kinsmen came from all over for the happy occasion.

As the guests gathered, an ugly old man came out of the crowd. He walked straight over to Papa.

Hábogi: I am Hábogi. And Helga will marry me.

Narrator: Papa could not bear the thought of giving his young daughter to such a dreadful-looking creature. Yet the man was so persuasive that Papa couldn't seem to reject him.

Papa: Off with you, man. I cannot make a decision yet. The wedding is about to begin.

Hábogi: Very well. But when the wedding is over, Helga will leave with me.

Act II

Narrator: The wedding of Inga to Sigmund and Marta to Sigurd took place. Afterward, the two older sisters discussed Helga and Hábogi. They had always been jealous of Helga. So they were happy to think that Helga might marry the horrible old man.

Inga: Your Sigurd is much handsomer than that awful Hábogi.

Marta: As is your Sigmund!

Inga: Poor, dear Helga. How sad that she will end up with that beast!

Narrator: Inga's words hung in the air for a moment. Then the sisters laughed merrily and skipped back to the party.

Act III

Narrator: After the wedding feast, Hábogi led a fine horse out of a nearby field. The horse had a brilliant saddle of crimson and gold. Helga looked at Hábogi's homely grin. Then quite against her wishes, she found herself jumping onto the saddle. Then Hábogi himself mounted the horse. He sat in front of Helga and took the reins.

Helga: Where are you taking me?

Hábogi: Don't worry. You'll see your family again.

Helga: That's no answer.

Hábogi: I am about to show you your new home. I hope you will be pleased.

Narrator: Soon, the couple had ridden out of sight. Mama and Papa were alarmed. But a strange force kept them from going after their sweet daughter.

Mama: I pray she will be safe.

Papa: Her future husband will protect her.

Narrator: Meanwhile, Hábogi and Helga's horse galloped across the country. They entered a meadow that had the greenest grass Helga had ever seen.

Helga: Oh, my! Look over there at those fluffy white sheep!

Hábogi: The finest sheep in the herd shall be yours. For this is my meadow—and my herd.

Narrator: Helga was stunned. She thanked Hábogi for his gift. Then they rode through a huge field. It was filled with the most charming gray cows imaginable.

Helga: The milk from those pretty cows must be delicious.

Hábogi: You are right. And after we wed, you shall taste the sweetest milk from the finest cow every morning. For this is my field. And these are my cows.

Narrator: Helga was impressed. But she remained silent. When they reached a valley, Helga nearly sprang out of the saddle. She shrieked with delight when she saw dozens of happy horses at play. There were horses of shiny chestnut, snow white, jet black, and golden yellow.

Helga: Tell me, Hábogi. Do you own these magnificent horses too?

Hábogi: Indeed, I do. Which one do you admire most?

Helga: They are all so lovely. But I would have to choose the jet-black one with the little white star on his forehead. Surely, Hábogi, you don't mean to give me a lamb, a cow, *and* a horse!

Hábogi: Ah, but surely I do. For you are to be my wife. And what's mine is yours.

Narrator: Helga didn't know *what* to think anymore. She was no longer afraid of Hábogi. However, she couldn't stop thinking about his face. It was so ugly. Hábogi had caught her staring at him. But he never shrank from her gaze. He just kept guiding the horse farther and farther into the country.

Many miles later, Hábogi stopped the horse in front of a tiny run-down shack. Helga did not like the looks of it.

Helga: Are we lost?

Hábogi: Not at all. This is my home. Soon it will be your home too.

Narrator: Now, Helga was sure that Hábogi had tricked her. She had believed that he owned all those sheep and cows and horses. But when she looked at the hut before her, she feared the worst.

Hábogi led Helga up the steps and through the door. Once she was inside, Helga's jaw dropped. She was blinded by the sparkling beauty of all that surrounded her. There were gold statues and silver baubles. Porcelain figurines and crystal vases. And silk tapestries and cushions. It was too much for Helga to take in.

Hábogi interrupted Helga's thoughts.

Hábogi: It is time for you to go. I must prepare for our wedding. My servant will take you home. In three days, he will bring you back with your family and your guests.

Narrator: Helga went with the servant. Her mind raced as they traveled back over the countryside. In no time, she was home.

Papa: My dear, dear girl!

Mama: You've come home to us!

Inga: Where is your Hábogi?

Marta: Let me guess—he's cast you aside.

Helga: I came home to invite you to my wedding. It's in three days.

Papa: But where is Hábogi from?

Mama: And what does he do?

Inga: What is he worth?

Marta: Do you realize how ugly your children will be?

Helga: You shall learn the answers you seek in three days. I promise.

Act IV

Narrator: Three days seemed forever to Inga and Marta. The sisters tried everything to get Helga to talk of her time with Hábogi. They asked sweetly. They tried trickery. They even begged. But Helga wouldn't say a word.

Finally, the wedding day arrived. And Helga's party set out for the celebration. Along the way, Helga pointed out Hábogi's sheep and cows and horses. Inga and Marta were positively green with envy. But the sight of Hábogi's awful-looking little hut did much to console them.

Inga: Well, well! What have we here?

Marta: What a *charming* little cottage! We're both so happy for you. Aren't we, Inga?

Inga: Naturally!

Narrator: The party moved inside, though. And the sisters were shocked. Never had they seen such finery.

Mama and Papa were delighted. They were convinced that Helga would have a good life with Hábogi. The sisters, though, were upset. They could not stand to think that Helga had found a better match than they had. And they were terribly jealous of Helga's beautiful, glittering wedding gown.

So that night, while the rest of the wedding party slept, Marta and Inga came up with a plan.

Marta: Helga does not deserve that dress!

Inga: How true! We can't let her look better than we did at our wedding.

Marta: What should we do?

Inga: We'll destroy her gown. It's the only way.

Narrator: By moonlight, the sisters took the dress outside. They hurled the gown into a pit and covered it with ashes.

Inga: No one will ever find this.

Marta: No one.

Narrator: Hábogi had seen the way Marta and Inga treated Helga. He sensed that they were up to no good. So he had kept an eye on them. And at the proper moment, he cast a spell that turned the ashes in the pit to rose petals. The sisters saw this, and they tried to run away. But it was too late. Hábogi had cast a spell over them too. They froze in place and were covered with ashes.

The next morning, the rest of the guests arrived for the wedding. Most just pointed and laughed at Marta and Inga.

A glorious castle was standing where the awful little hut had been. Helga and a handsome prince stood in front of it. The prince wore a splendid coat of blue velvet and silver trim. And Helga was radiant in her beautiful gown. Mama and Papa rushed to Helga's side.

Mama and Papa: Who is this man?

Helga: This is my Hábogi.